PRIMARY SOURCES
IMMIGRATION AND MIGRATION
★ IN AMERICA ★

NATIVE AMERICAN MIGRATION

Tracee Sioux

The Rosen Publishing Group's

PowerKids Press
PRIMARY SOURCE

New York

To Staci Duke, my soul sister, Ainsley's Fairy Godmother and the best ⅛ Indian I know

Published in 2004 by The Rosen Publishing Group, Inc.
29 East 21st Street, New York, NY 10010

Copyright © 2004 by The Rosen Publishing Group, Inc.

First Edition

Editor: Rachel O'Connor
Book Design: Emily Muschinske

Photo Credits: Cover and title page, p. 7 (left) Smithsonian American Art Museum, Washington, D.C./Art Resource, NY; p. 4 Eric DePalo; p. 7 (top) Photo Researchers, Inc.; p. 7 (right) Joslyn Art Museum, Omaha, Nebraska; p. 8 (top) Edward Lamson Henry (1841–1919), Johnson Hall, oil on canvas, 1903, Albany Institute of History and Art; pp. 8 (bottom), 12 (bottom) National Archives and Records Administration; p. 11 (top) courtesy of Oregon Historical Society, Portland (OrHi 101538, OrHi 101540); p. 11 (bottom) Emily Muschinske; p 12 (top) courtesy Frank H. McClung Museum, The University of Tennessee. Painting by Carlyle Urello; p. 15 Woolaroc Museum, Bartlesville, Oklahoma; pp. 16 (top), 16 (left), 20 © Hulton/Archive/Getty Images; p 16 (bottom) © Corbis; p. 19 (top) Southwest Museum; p. 19 (bottom) © Bettmann/Corbis.

Comanche Village, women dressing robes and drying meat, 1834–35, by George Catlin. A detail of this painting is reproduced on page 7.

Sioux, Tracee.
Native American migration / Tracee Sioux.— 1st ed.
    v. cm. — (Primary sources of immigration and migration in America)
Includes bibliographical references and index.
Contents: The first immigrants — Indian nations — Native Americans and European immigrants — The formation of the United States — Native American migration — Cherokee Nation and the Trail of Tears — More migrations — Bloodshed and loss — Battle of Little Bighorn — Indian reservations today.
ISBN 0-8239-6825-1 (lib. bdg.) — ISBN 0-8239-8951-8 (pbk.)
1. Indians of North America—Relocation—Juvenile literature. 2. Indians of North America—Migrations—Juvenile literature. [1. Indians of North America—Relocation. 2. Indians of North America—Migrations. 3. Migration, Internal.] I. Title. II. Series.
E98.R4 S56 2004
973.04'97—dc21
                        2003000749

Manufactured in the United States of America

Contents

Asia

Arctic Ocean

Site of
Bering
Land Bridge

Greenland

Northwest
Coast

Subarctic

Pacific Ocean

Rocky Mountains

Northeast

Great
Basin

Great
Plains

Atlantic Ocean

California

Southeast

Southwest

The First Immigrants

The Native Americans, or Indians, were the first immigrants to settle in the Americas. Historians believe that Indians emigrated from Asia about 20,000 to 30,000 years ago. By the time the Europeans started to colonize America in the 1500s, there were probably millions of Native Americans in North America and South America. When Christopher Columbus landed in the Americas in 1492, he believed he had found India. He called the people he saw Indios, which is Spanish for "Indians." European colonization forced thousands of Native Americans to migrate from their settlements to other parts of America.

This map shows the many migration routes the Native Americans might have taken as they settled throughout the Americas. They are believed to have crossed the Bering Land Bridge from Asia into North America.

Indian Nations

Before the arrival of the European immigrants, Native Americans lived in all parts of America. Early Native Americans roamed the land and settled in places where they found good hunting or fertile land to grow crops. The Indian nations that settled in the southeastern parts of North America, such as the Cherokee and the Seminole, lived mostly in log homes. They hunted, gathered wild fruits and vegetables, and also farmed. The Native Americans of the Great Plains, such as the Sioux, moved around following the herds of buffalo they hunted. They lived in tepees. Indian nations in the Southwest, such as the Apache and the Navajo, were mostly farming nations.

Left: This painting by George Catlin shows a Comanche village. The Comanche were skilled horsemen who moved around the southern Plains.

The Pomeiooc in Virginia lived in open-sided homes made with wood poles and moss or bark.

Above: Mato-Tope was chief of the Mandan. Most of his people died from smallpox, an illness brought by Europeans.

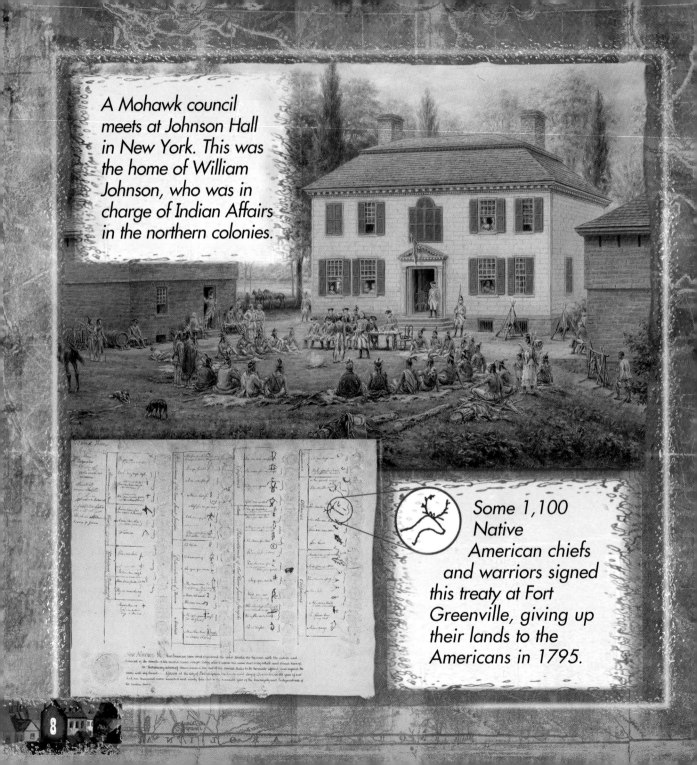

A Mohawk council meets at Johnson Hall in New York. This was the home of William Johnson, who was in charge of Indian Affairs in the northern colonies.

Some 1,100 Native American chiefs and warriors signed this treaty at Fort Greenville, giving up their lands to the Americans in 1795.

Native Americans and European Immigrants

The British started to colonize the East Coast in the late 1500s. However, Native Americans had already settled in some of the areas where the British immigrants wanted to live. From the beginning, relations between the colonists and the Native Americans were strained. Among other things, they had very different ideas about the land. The Indians did not think that land could be owned by one person. It was there for everyone to share. The Europeans, however, wanted to own the land. They did not want to share it with the Indians and became angry when Indians used land that colonists believed was theirs. Indians were angry that Europeans settled anywhere they liked without talking it over with the Indians.

The Formation of the United States

In 1776, the British immigrants living in the 13 colonies on the East Coast declared their independence and formed the United States of America. In 1803, the president of the United States, Thomas Jefferson, bought the French-owned Louisiana Territory, more than doubling the size of America. Jefferson sent an expedition led by Meriwether Lewis and William Clark to find a passage that connected the Atlantic Ocean to the Pacific Ocean. They left in May 1804. On their travels west, whenever they met Native American settlers, Lewis and Clark would tell them that their land now belonged to the United States.

This map shows the route taken by Lewis and Clark. It also shows the Louisiana Purchase, in which more than 885,000 square miles (2,292,139.5 sq km) of land were bought for $15 million.

Inset: *Items such as this Thomas Jefferson peace medal were given to Indians as friendship gifts. The medal shows Jefferson on one side and shaking hands on the other.*

Above: Cherokee Indians lived in several states in southeastern America. They built homes and farms, like the one shown here. Their children went to missionary schools. They did not want to give up their homes and move west.

Left: Shown here is the Indian Removal Act of 1830.

Native American Migration

   Although the United States expanded westward, many Americans did not want to settle in this region. The Americans did want to remove the Native Americans from their eastern territory, though. In 1830, the government introduced the Indian Removal Act, whereby the Indian nations would be given unsettled land west of the Mississippi River in exchange for their eastern lands. Many Native American nations in the Northeast agreed to sign over their land and settled peacefully in western lands. However, not all Indian nations were eager to resettle, especially those in the Southeast. Nations such as the Cherokee, the Seminole, and the Creek refused to leave the land on which they had settled.

The Cherokee Nation and the Trail of Tears

The Indian Removal Act allowed Americans to use force to remove the remaining Indian nations from the East. One example of this use of force involved the Cherokee nation. The Cherokee did not want to move west. They refused to leave their homes. In the summer of 1838, the U.S. Army came to round up the Cherokee. They forced thousands of Cherokee Indians to march west. Many of the Indians died on the trail, which was about 800 miles (1,287.5 km) long. It is known as the Trail of Tears. The Cherokee reached their destination, which was the Indian territory in the West that is now Oklahoma, by March 1839.

This painting by Robert Lindneux, called Trail of Tears, *shows the hardships the Cherokee endured when they were forced from their homes in the East.*

Right: Native Americans are shown here trying to destroy part of the Union Pacific Railroad.

In attempts to keep their homes, Native Americans sometimes attacked white settlers. Here, in an 1890 print, Indians attack a wagon train.

GRAND RUSH
FOR THE
INDIAN
TERRITORY !

Over 15,000,000 Acres of Land
NOW OPEN FOR SETTLEMENT !

Being part of the Land bought by the Government in 1866 from the Indians for the Freedmen.

NOW IS THE CHANCE
TO
PROCURE A HOME
In this Beautiful Country !

THE FINEST TIMBER !
THE RICHEST LAND !
THE FINEST WATERED !
WEST OF THE MISSISSIPPI RIVER.

Every person over 21 years of age is entitled to receive, either by pre-emption or homestead, who wishes to settle in the Indian Territory. It is estimated that over Fifty Thousand will move to this Territory in the next ninety days. The Indians are rejoicing to have the whites settle up this country.

The Grand Expedition will Leave Independence May 7, 1879

Independence is situated at the terminus of the Kansas City, Lawrence & Southern Railroad. The citizens of Independence have laid out and made a splendid road to these lands; and they are prepared to furnish emigrants with complete outfits, such as wagons, agricultural implements, dry goods, groceries, lumber and stock. They have also opened an office there for general information to those wishing to go to the Territory. IT COSTS NOTHING TO BECOME A MEMBER OF THIS COLONY!

Persons passing through Kansas City will apply at the office of K. C. L. & S. R. R. opposite Union Depot, for Tickets.

ABOUT THE LANDS.

[fine print paragraphs about the lands]

DISTANCES FROM INDEPENDENCE.

[table of distances]

ADDRESS
WM. C. BRANHAM,
Independence, Kansas.

More Migrations

The number of immigrants coming to America began to grow quite quickly. This was particularly true in the 1840s and during the California gold rush, which began in 1848. This growth meant that American citizens started to move west, using such routes as the Oregon Trail, the Mormon Trail, and the Santa Fe Trail. The building of the Union and Central Railroads in the 1860s allowed even greater numbers of people to travel west. All this meant trouble for the Native Americans, who once again were settled on land that the Americans now wanted. However, this time many of the Indian nations fought violently against the Americans who were trying to take their land.

Right: Advertisements such as this one tried to bring new people west by offering land owned by the Indians.

Battle of the Little Bighorn

One of the biggest Native American victories over whites in the West was the Battle of the Little Bighorn in 1876. It involved the Cheyenne and the Sioux who were settled in Dakota Territory. This land had been given to them by the U.S. government. However, as the search for gold continued in the West, white miners began to settle on this land. After several fights between the Native Americans and the gold miners, the U.S. Army's Seventh Cavalry, led by General George Armstrong Custer, was sent to force the Indians to a reservation. Custer, however, underestimated his foes. His entire group was killed in the battle, often called Custer's Last Stand.

Indian chief Kicking Bear created this painting, showing the Battle of the Little Bighorn, in 1876.

Tatanka Iyotanka, or Sitting Bull, was the leader of the Hunkpapa Lakota Sioux. He united the Lakota in their fight against the Americans trying to take over the land.

Bloodshed and Loss

During the second half of the nineteenth century, the U.S. settlers and the Native Americans had many violent battles. Even though the Native Americans celebrated some victories, in the end they lost huge numbers of their people and all of their land. As the U.S. government took more and more land from the Indians, it set aside areas of land, called reservations, for Indian settlement. By the end of the 1800s, after much bloodshed and loss, most Native Americans had been moved to reservations in the West. The Battle of Wounded Knee in 1890 was the last major defeat of the Native Americans.

Here a Native American woman sits beneath a funeral platform, mourning the death of a warrior at the Battle of Wounded Knee.

Indian Reservations Today

Today there are about 280 federal and state Indian reservations, on which almost half of the 2.5 million Native Americans now live. The largest reservation covers 14 million acres (5.7 million ha) in Arizona, New Mexico, and Utah. More than 150,000 Navajo Indians live there today. Most reservations are less than 1,000 acres (404.7 ha) and some are less than 100 acres (40.5 ha). Farming is the most common occupation for Indians on reservations. Though life continues to be difficult for many Indians, they have worked hard to keep their culture and traditions. Their part in American history, though at times a sad one, is an example of spirit and courage, traits that Americans value so highly.

Glossary

cavalry (KA-vul-ree) The part of an army that rides and fights on horseback.

council (KOWN-sul) A group that discusses or settles questions.

culture (KUL-chur) The beliefs and practices of a group of people.

declared (dih-KLERD) Announced officially.

defeat (dih-FEET) A loss.

destination (des-tih-NAY-shun) A place to which a person travels.

difficult (DIH-fih-kult) Hard to do or understand.

emigrated (EM-uh-grayt-ed) To have left one country to settle in another.

expanded (ek-SPAND-ed) Spread out, or grew larger.

fertile (FER-tul) Good for making and growing things.

hardships (HARD-ships) Events or actions that cause suffering.

immigrants (IH-muh-grints) People who move to a new country from another country.

occupation (ah-kyoo-PAY-shun) The kind of work a person does to make a living.

reservation (reh-zer-VAY-shun) An area of land set aside by the government for Native Americans to live on.

traditions (truh-DIH-shunz) Ways of doing things that have been passed down over time.

traits (TRAYTS) Features that make people special.

underestimated (un-dur-ES-tih-mayt-ed) Placed too low a value on.

violently (VY-lent-lee) Using strong, rough force.

Index

Primary Sources

Cover. *Young Omahaw, War Eagle, Little Missouri, and Pawnees.* Oil on canvas. By Charles Bird King. 1821. Gift of Helen Barlow to the Smithsonian American Art Museum. **Page 7. Top center.** Pomeiooc. A typical Indian settlement in Virginia during the 1500s. Sketch by John White, who is believed to have been born circa 1540, and to have died circa 1606. **Bottom left.** *Comanche Village, Women dressing robes and drying meat.* By George Catlin. 1834–1835. **Right.** Mato-Tope (Four Bears). Mandan Chief. By Karl Bodmer (1809–1893). From the Joslyn Art Museum, Omaha. **Page 8. Bottom.** Treaty at Fort Greenville. 1795. A treaty of peace between the United States and the groups of Indians called the Wyandot, Delaware, Shawnee, Ottawa, and others. Under the treaty, the Indian nations ceded pieces of land to the United States. **Page 11. Inset.** Thomas Jefferson Peace Medal of 1801. This silver medallion has the image of Thomas Jefferson on one side, and clasped hands and crossed pipes on the other. **Page 12.** The Indian Removal Act, 1830. **Page 16. Top center.** Native Americans creep out of the tall grass at night and sabotage the track of the Union Pacific as a train approaches. Circa 1855. **Right.** An advertisement for Native American land that has been made available to settlers. From a Kansas City, Missouri, newspaper, 1879. **Page 19. Top.** *Battle of the Little Bighorn.* By Kicking Bear. 1898. **Bottom.** Photograph of Sitting Bull, taken in 1885. **Page 20.** A Native American woman sits beneath a burial platform and mourns for a slain warrior shortly after the massacre at Wounded Knee. Published in *Harper's Weekly*, 1891.

Web Sites

Due to the changing nature of Internet links, PowerKids Press has developed an online list of Web sites related to the subject of this book. This site is updated regularly. Please use this link to access the list:
www.powerkidslinks.com/psima/native/